EPPING

SPACE
PIONEERS

ROBIN KERROD

WORLD ALMANAC® LIBRARY

Please visit our web site at:
www.worldalmanaclibrary.com
For a free color catalog describing
World Almanac® Library's list of high-quality
books and multimedia programs, call
1-800-848-2928 (USA) or 1-800-387-3178
(Canada). World Almanac® Library's fax:
(414) 332-3567.

Library of Congress Cataloging-in-Publication Data

Kerrod, Robin.
    Space pioneers / by Robin Kerrod.
       p. cm. — (The history of space exploration)
    Includes bibliographical references and index.
    ISBN 0-8368-5707-0 (lib. bdg.)
    ISBN 0-8368-5714-3 (softcover)
       1. Manned space flight—History—Juvenile
    literature. I. Title. II. Series.
    TL793.H459   2004
    629.45'009—dc22   2004048040

    First published in 2005 by
    World Almanac® Library
    330 West Olive Street, Suite 100
    Milwaukee, WI 53212 USA

    Copyright © 2005 by World
    Almanac® Library.

Developed by White-Thomson Publishing Ltd
Editor: Veronica Ross
Designer: Gary Frost, Leishman Design
Picture researcher: Elaine Fuoco-Lang

World Almanac® Library editor: Carol Ryback
World Almanac® Library designer: Kami Koenig
World Almanac® Library art direction: Tammy West

Photo credits: top (t), bottom (b), left (l), right (r)
All images used with the permission of NASA
except: Bettmann/CORBIS 7; Robin Kerrod/Space
Charts 8(b), 9(b), 10, 11, 21, 25(bl), 25(r), 26(bl),
29(t), 30, 34, 35(t), 37(r), 42; Rex Features 26.
Illustrations by Peter Bull.

Printed in Canada

1 2 3 4 5 6 7 8 9 09 08 07 06 05 04

Cover: The "Original 7" astronauts selected for the Mercury program in 1959.

Title page: An Agena rocket target vehicle for the Gemini 9 mission.

Contents page: Alan Shepard is winched to safety after his flight in Freedom 7.

◀ Gemini 4 *blasts into space June 3, 1965.*

CONTENTS

BLAZING TRAILS

Even before the Space Age began with the flight of *Sputnik* in October 1957, many anticipated the next stage in the conquest of space—human spaceflight. And in less than four years, both the Soviet Union and the United States had launched people into space. The U.S. called its space travelers astronauts; the Soviets, cosmonauts.

▲ Gemini 4 *astronaut Edward White tumbles head over heels as he makes the first U.S. space walk on June 3, 1965.*

Before the human conquest of space began,
no one knew whether or not human beings could survive
a flight into space. The flights of the pioneering astronauts proved that
they can. On October 7, 1958, just six days after its formation, the National
Aeronautics and Space Administration (NASA) announced the first man-in-space program,
called Mercury. President Dwight D. Eisenhower decided that NASA should choose its astronauts
from the ranks of the U.S. military services. Early the following year, NASA asked the U.S. military services
for the names of potential pilots for the Mercury spacecraft. Only the best of the best need apply: First of
all, the men (and at that time, it was only men) had to be extremely fit; they needed an engineering
degree; they also had to be test pilots. And, each one could not stand more than than 5 feet 11 inches
(180 centimeters) tall—in order to fit inside the Mercury spacecraft.

An initial screening of a list of five hundred was whittled down to thirty-two. After intensive medical
and psychological testing, seven finalists remained. NASA presented the "Original 7" astronauts—
L. Gordon Cooper, Virgil I. "Gus" Grissom, and Donald K. "Deke" Slayton (all air force), John H. Glenn Jr.
(marines), and M. Scott Carpenter, Walter M. "Wally" Schirra, and Alan B. Shepard Jr. (all navy)—to the
world at a press conference on April 9, 1959.

Also in 1959, the Soviet Union called for air force test pilots to train as cosmonauts. Hundreds applied,
but just twenty made the final cut after undergoing physical and psychological testing.

CHAPTER ONE

VOSTOK AND MERCURY

The Soviet Vostok and U.S. Mercury programs that led the human exploration of the space frontier shared similar goals: to place a manned spacecraft in orbit, to investigate man's ability to function in space, and to recover the man and the spacecraft safely.

In the Soviet Union, chief designer Sergei Korolev had been working on designs for manned spacecraft since 1958. He got the okay from the Soviet Academy of Sciences to build one in November 1959. The Soviets named their craft *Vostok* ("East").

Vostok's design allowed for only one passenger. The spacecraft consisted of two parts. The cosmonaut traveled in a spherical reentry capsule that measured just 90 inches (2.3 meters) in diameter. He rode

▶ *A cutaway of the Vostok spacecraft. The cosmonaut rode in the spherical reentry capsule, which measured 7.5 feet (2.3 m) in diameter. This separated from the 10-foot (3-m) -long equipment module before reentry. The craft had a mass of about 10,500 pounds (4,700 kilograms).*

Communications antenna

Command control antenna

Reentry capsule

Porthole

Cosmonaut

Ejection seat

Oxygen and nitrogen bottles

Whip antenna

Equipment module

Communications antenna

Retrorocket

strapped into an ejection seat so that he could eject during a liftoff emergency or just before landing.

Spacecraft use atmospheric braking when returning from space. A heat shield, consisting of a thick layer of material designed to melt away as the capsule plunges back into the increasingly thicker atmosphere, covers the outside. This insulating layer protects the passenger from the extreme heat of reentry.

An equipment module made up the second part of Vostok. It carried oxygen and nitrogen bottles and sets of little rockets called thrusters. These thrusters controlled the attitude, or orientation, of the capsule in space. The equipment module also carried a larger retrorocket. Aimed in the opposite direction to which the capsule traveled in orbit, the firing of the retrorocket (the retrobraking maneuver) near the end of a mission decreased the speed of the capsule enough to drop it from orbit so that gravity would pull it back to Earth.

The first flight of a Vostok spacecraft, with a dummy cosmonaut on board, took place on May 15, 1960, from the Baikonur Cosmodrome in Kazakhstan. Two weeks earlier, a U.S. U-2 spy plane (piloted by Francis Gary Powers) had photographed the Vostok on the launchpad before he and his plane were shot down.

Later in 1960, and in early 1961, the Soviets sent dogs into orbit in Vostok spacecraft before attempting the first manned spaceflight. The dogs flew in Vostok capsules, but the Soviets did not begin numbering their spacecraft until the first manned missions.

▶ *U2 pilot Francis Gary Powers holds a model of the plane he flew. Sentenced to ten years by a Soviet court for spying, Powers was released in 1962 in exchange for convicted Soviet spy Rudolf Abel.*

THE U-2 AFFAIR

On May 1, 1960, a Soviet missile shot down U.S. Air Force Lieutenant Francis Gary Powers' U-2 reconnaissance plane. Powers bailed out and was captured as a spy. Part of his mission was to photograph the new Soviet Vostok "on the pad" at Baikonur, Kazakhstan. Soviet Premier Nikita Khrushchev stormed out of a summit meeting held two weeks later in Paris, France, when U.S. President Dwight D. Eisenhower refused to apologize for the incident. The Soviets imprisoned Powers for twenty-one months. They traded him for Soviet spy Colonel Rudolph Ivanovich Abel.

MERCURY

In 1959, while engineers finalized the design of the Mercury capsule, the astronauts began their training. Unmanned test flights of the Redstone and Atlas launch vehicles occurred at Cape Canaveral, Florida, in 1960.

A chimpanzee named Ham flew in a Mercury capsule launched into suborbital flight by a Redstone rocket in January 1961. His successful mission led to the first U.S. manned suborbital flights later in the year. (A suborbital flight is one in which a spacecraft arcs into space and falls back to Earth without going into orbit.)

▲ *The seven Mercury astronauts during a survival course at Stead Air Force Base in Nevada in 1960, practicing for possible emergency landings. From left to right, they are Gordon Cooper, Scott Carpenter, John Glenn, Alan Shepard, Gus Grissom, Wally Schirra, and Donald Slayton. Slayton was the only man who did not fly in the Mercury program.*

▼ *Technicians fit astronaut Gordon Cooper into what will become the couch on his Mercury spacecraft. The tiny Mercury capsules left little room for astronauts to move.*

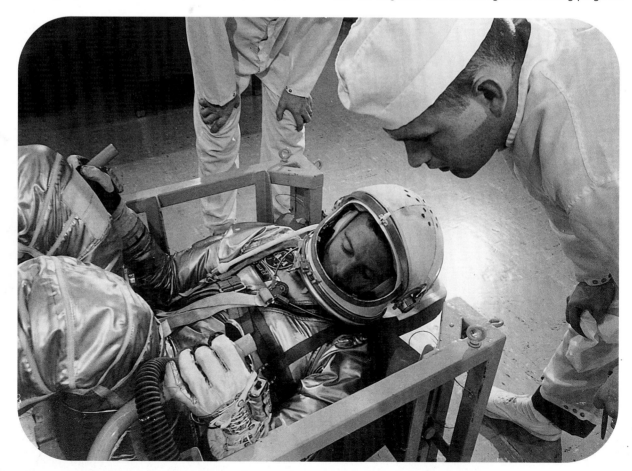

THE MERCURY CAPSULE

The U.S. bell-shaped Mercury spacecraft was usually referred to as a capsule. Size and shape considerations limited its dimensions because it needed to fit on top of the Redstone and Atlas rockets that would boost it into space.

The capsule measured 9.5 feet (2.9 m) high and about 6 feet (1.8 m) across at the base. Its escape tower had a rocket motor that would fire and lift the capsule clear of the launch rocket during a liftoff emergency. Inside the capsule, straps held the astronaut in his shaped seat. He sat with his back to the base of the craft. This position placed his back to the launch rockets, enabling him to better withstand the G-forces of acceleration during liftoff.

The Mercury capsule held all the equipment necessary to operate the craft and to keep the astronaut alive. Retrorockets were strapped to the heat shield at the base of the craft.

▼ A Mercury spacecraft under construction. It was built mainly of nickel alloy with an outer layer of heat-resistant titanium as added protection against the heat of reentry.

G-FORCES

When astronauts are launched into space, their carrier rocket accelerates rapidly, going from 0 to 17,500 miles per hour (0 to 28,000 kilometers per hour) in a matter of minutes. The forces—known as G-forces—on their bodies created by this fierce acceleration are several times greater than the normal force of Earth's gravity. Astronauts also experience increased G-forces when they return from space as their craft brakes rapidly while it plunges back into the atmosphere. In the early days of space flight, astronauts endured forces of 10 Gs or more. Space Shuttle astronauts experience maximum forces of about 3 Gs. A Space Shuttle's acceleration force is less fierce because the enormous craft take longer to build up speed.

▼ A Mercury capsule being lifted onto the recovery ship after a flight into space. The heat shield and landing air bag at the base was lowered and inflated to cushion the impact of splashdown. All U.S. spacecraft, Mercury through Apollo, splashed down at sea.

AUTOMATIC CONTROL

Sets of jet thrusters fired in the appropriate direction controlled the attitude, or orientation, of the capsule in space. The thrusters were designed to fire automatically, but if necessary, the astronauts could take over with a manual override. Most of the time, though, the Mercury flights were under automatic control, a condition the astronauts called the "Spam in the can" approach.

LIFE SUPPORT

Life support is the most essential system in any spacecraft. It must supply oxygen at the correct pressure for the astronauts to breathe in, and it must remove the carbon dioxide as they breathe out. In addition, the life-support system should remove odors and keep the spacecraft atmosphere at a pleasant temperature using a kind of air conditioner.

Soviet spacecraft used a mixture of nitrogen and oxygen in their life-support systems to simulate ordinary air. The U.S. spacecraft—Mercury through Apollo—relied on pure oxygen. Space Shuttles, however, use a nitrogen/oxygen combination.

MESSY BUSINESS

There are, of course, less pleasant aspects to life support aboard a spacecraft, particularly "waste management." Astronauts on an extended flight must cope with going to the bathroom in space. The lack of gravity to remove body wastes presents the biggest problem. Mercury astronauts urinated into a bag inside their flight suit. Their low-fiber diet before a flight helped lessen the chances of the need for bowel movements. On the longer Gemini

▼ The centrifuge early astronauts used to get used to the increased G-forces they would experience during launch and reentry. They were strapped into a cabin (seen on the left) that traveled in a circle at the end of a long rotating arm. The centrifugal forces on the astronaut's body set up by the rotation mimicked the G-forces of space flight.

▲ *Gemini astronaut Edwin Aldrin practices for space walking in a huge water tank called a neutral buoyancy chamber. He wears a suit similar to a space suit. It is perfectly weighted so that he neither rises nor sinks in the water. This reproduces the conditions of weightlessness experienced in orbiting spacecraft.*

and Apollo missions, the astronauts used fecal bags that they attached to their buttocks with sticky tape. But in the confines of their capsule, emptying their bowels and bladder was no easy—or pleasant—task.

SUITED UP

Although the insides of the Mercury and Gemini crew capsules were pressurized—supplied with oxygen under normal atmospheric pressure—the astronauts also wore space suits that would save their lives if the capsules sprung a leak.

The two-layered Mercury space suit was modeled after the U.S. Navy Mark IV flight suit worn by high-altitude test pilots. An outer restraint layer prevented the inner layer (which could be pressurized with oxygen in an emergency) from ballooning. Its silvery, aluminized outer finish reflected heat.

As space exploration continued and the missions became more complicated, the space suits evolved to fit the requirements of those missions. For example, while the Mercury astronauts simply sat in one place in their capsules, the Gemini astronauts needed more flexible space suits with better joints to help them maneuver outside the capsule.

The more substantial Gemini suit also included extra cover layers that provided greater protection from space hazards such as meteorite particles, cosmic rays, and extremes of heat during space walks (extra-vehicular activities, or EVAs).

CHAPTER TWO

A MOMENTOUS YEAR

In 1961, both the Soviet Union and the United States made their first manned voyages into space. On May 25, 1961, President John F. Kennedy urged the United States to head for the Moon.

▲ Cosmonaut Yuri Gagarin rests before his historic spaceflight on April 12, 1961. He orbited Earth once aboard Vostok 1. The entire world hailed his bravery.

By the beginning of 1961, both the Soviet Union and the United States had the hardware necessary to begin the human push into space. The Soviet Union had the Vostok spacecraft and A-series rocket; the United States had the Mercury spacecraft and Redstone rocket. Only a few last-minute tests remained.

Chimpanzee Ham's successful suborbital flight on a Mercury-Redstone on January 31, 1961, was a dress rehearsal for an upcoming U.S. manned suborbital flight. On March 9 and March 25, the Soviet Union put *Sputnik 9* and *Sputnik 10* into orbit. Both carried dogs that returned safely to Earth. The Soviets had mastered the techniques of orbiting living things and returning them home safely. Now it was a person's turn.

FIRST MAN IN SPACE

In the early morning of April 11, 1961, a launch rocket with a Vostok spacecraft on top was rolled out to the launchpad at the Baikonur Cosmodrome. For the next twenty-four hours, the pad was a scene of hectic activity as technicians readied the rocket for liftoff.

◄ A Mercury-Redstone rocket stands on the launchpad at Cape Canaveral, Florida. It was 83 feet (25.3 m) tall and had a launch weight of about 66,000 pounds (29,960 kg). Mercury-Redstones launched animals and astronauts on suborbital flights—flights in which they traveled only briefly in space and did not go into orbit.

About 7:30 A.M. Moscow time on April 12, an orange-suited figure rode an elevator 100 feet (30 m) to the top of the rocket and climbed into the spacecraft, *Vostok 1*. He was Yuri Gagarin, a pilot in the Soviet Air Force. The countdown ticked away, and at 9:07 A.M. Moscow time, the engines of the mighty rocket ignited and lifted the launch vehicle off the pad.

In his capsule, Gagarin heard the deafening roar of the engines, felt juddering vibrations, and began to sense the G-forces on his body mounting as the launch vehicle accelerated. But after about eight minutes, the rockets cut out and separated. Now there was no noise, no vibrations, no G-forces. Gagarin was in orbit about 113 miles (181 km) above Earth, traveling nearly 5 miles (8 km) every second. *Vostok 1* sped over Siberia toward the Pacific Ocean, which it crossed in just twenty minutes. It went south of Cape

Horn, Argentina, then across the southern Atlantic, over Africa, and back toward Gagarin's homeland.

During this time, Gagarin reported that weightlessness was not a problem. As he sailed around high above Earth, he practiced eating and drinking. He commented on the awesome views of Earth through the porthole and the abrupt color changes as day turned to night and night to day again as he passed into and out of Earth's shadow.

> "I saw for the first time the spherical shape of the Earth. You can see its curvature when looking to the horizon. It is unique and beautiful. Of all the nights I had seen in my lifetime, none was remotely comparable to night in space. The stars were so clearly visible—blindingly bright and full-bodied. The sky was blacker than it ever appears from the Earth, with the real slate-blackness of space."
>
> **Yuri Gagarin after his pioneering space flight in 1961.**

BACK TO EARTH

Gagarin could not control *Vostok 1*. It flew in automatic mode according to a preplanned program. Over Africa, the spacecraft's retrorockets fired to slow it down. The instrument section and reentry capsule separated. As the capsule plunged back into the atmosphere, heat shield blazing, Gagarin felt the G-forces build up again.

Atmospheric braking quickly slowed the craft. At a height of about 5 miles (8 km), Gagarin ejected from the craft in his ejection seat and began descending by parachute. He jettisoned the seat itself at about 2.5 miles (4 km) altitude. Gagarin landed safely. His flight lasted 108 minutes. In a little more than an hour and a half, a human being had endured the punishing G-forces of a fiery liftoff, traveled weightless around the world in space, and survived unharmed through reentry into the atmosphere.

Radio Moscow had already made a historic announcement: "Today, 12 April 1961, the first cosmic ship named *Vostok*, with a man on board, was orbited around the Earth from the Soviet Union. He is an airman, Major Yuri Gagarin."

YURI GAGARIN (1934–1968)

The first man in space, Yuri Alexeyevich Gagarin was born near Smolensk in what is now Russia. He graduated from flying school in November 1957, shortly after the launch of *Sputnik 2*. Gagarin joined the Soviet Air Force as a Lieutenant and began cosmonaut training in 1960. He was promoted to major during his one-orbit flight, which was his only spaceflight. Tragically, he died in an airplane crash in March 1968. His ashes are interred in the Kremlin Wall on Red Square in Moscow.

▲ Before he climbs into his Mercury capsule, Freedom 7, on May 5, 1961, Alan Shepard talks with Gus Grissom, who will follow him into space two months later.

FREEDOM FLIGHT

Back in the United States, final preparations were underway at Cape Canaveral for a brief suborbital flight—the first U.S. manned space launch. Earlier attempts on May 2 and May 4, failed, but the countdown for a launch on May 5 went smoothly.

Early that morning, Alan Shepard climbed into his cramped Mercury capsule named *Freedom 7*. Shepard chose that name to emphasize the freedom his country enjoyed (compared to the lack of freedom in the Soviet Union). At 9:34 A.M. (local time), the vehicle lifted off the launchpad as the Redstone rocket's engines roared to life. They boosted it to a speed of nearly 5,200 miles per hour (8,400 kph) before cutting out after burning for about two-and-a-half minutes.

Inside, Shepard experienced forces of more than 6 Gs, with his heart pounding at a rate of nearly 140 beats a minute. *Freedom 7* separated from its

▼ Redstone rockets roar and thrust Freedom 7 into the sky on the morning of May 5, 1961. Inside, astronaut Alan Shepard readies himself to become the first American in space.

launch rocket and continued on a trajectory (flight path) that took it to a maximum altitude of 116 miles (187 km) above Earth.

MANUAL CONTROL

As *Freedom 7* soared in space, Shepard experienced weightlessness for a little less than five minutes. During this time, he briefly assumed manual control of the capsule. By firing *Freedom 7*'s altitude thrusters, Shepard demonstrated that an astronaut could control his craft in the vacuum of space.

As *Freedom 7* began its descent, Shepard fired its retrorockets to test the braking capabilities of the spacecraft. This was actually an unnecessary maneuver for Shepard's flight because his capsule never reached orbit. He therefore did not need to slow down to fall from orbit. It was only a test.

THE FLEA JUMP

Shepard's flight came to an end when the *Freedom 7* capsule descended by parachute and splashed down in the Atlantic Ocean 297 miles (478 km) from its launch site. Local time was 9:49 A.M. Shepard's flight had lasted just over fifteen minutes. Americans everywhere celebrated the historic achievement of the United States. In the Soviet Union however, premier Khrushchev dismissed the flight as a "flea jump."

KENNEDY'S PLEA

On May 8, at a ceremony at the White House, President Kennedy pinned a Distinguished Service

▼ *After his successful flight in* Freedom 7, *Alan Shepard is winched aboard a helicopter that will take him to the recovery ship, the USS* Lake Champlain. Freedom 7 *floats below Shepard on the Atlantic Ocean's surface.*

▲ President John F. Kennedy congratulates Alan Shepard after his pioneering flight into space.

Medal on Alan Shepard. Hours later, Vice President Lyndon B. Johnson presented Kennedy with a report recommending that he give a U.S. Moon landing the highest priority.

Kennedy enthusiastically agreed, and in a speech before Congress on May 25, he urged the United States to embark on one of the most exciting and daring projects ever attempted: to land on the Moon. His speech launched the Apollo Program.

> Space is open to us now, and our eagerness to share its meaning is not governed by the efforts of others. We go into space because whatever man must undertake, free men must fully share. I believe that this nation should commit itself to achieving the goal, before this decade is out, of landing a man on the Moon and returning him safely to Earth. . . . It will not be one man going to the Moon—it will be an entire nation.
> **President Kennedy addressing Congress on May 25, 1961.**

REPEAT PERFORMANCE

Two further manned flights took place in 1961 which demonstrated the enormous divide between the space efforts of the United States and the Soviet Union.

On July 21, Virgil ("Gus") Grissom flew in a Mercury capsule named *Liberty Bell 7* on a suborbital flight that was a repeat of Shepard's mission. But Grissom almost drowned when the spacecraft sank after splashdown.

Compare Grissom's fifteen-minute flight with that of Soviet cosmonaut Gherman Titov: He took off on August 6 and flew around the world seventeen times. His flight lasted more than twenty-five hours.

▲ Second U.S. astronaut in space Gus Grissom after his brief flight on July 21, 1961. He was recovered safely, but his capsule, Liberty Bell 7, was lost at sea until 1998.

CHAPTER THREE

THE END OF THE BEGINNING

U.S. astronauts eventually made it into orbit early in 1962, and both the United States and the Soviet Union ended their first programs of manned space exploration the following year. Still, the Soviet Union pulled ahead of the U.S. with dual flights—one of which included the first woman in space.

▲ *Soviet cosmonaut Gherman Titov was only twenty-five when he made the world's second spaceflight into orbit in August 1961. He became the first person to sleep in space—and the first to suffer from space sickness.*

Cosmonaut Gherman Titov's day-long flight in August 1961 naturally dismayed U.S. rocket scientists, who needed to carry out further test flights before they could launch an astronaut into orbit. They wanted to iron out any potential problems with the Mercury-Atlas 6, the upgraded launch vehicle they planned to use for orbital flight.

Successful orbital tests with a "simulated man" in September and then chimpanzee Enos in November were both successful. These procedures verified operational procedures, checked tracking networks, and tested communications systems.

THE LAUNCH OF *FRIENDSHIP*

Even before Enos's flight, the date for the first manned Mercury-Atlas 6 launch was scheduled for December 19, 1961. But this launch date became unrealistic when simulated countdown and flight tests took longer than anticipated. NASA postponed liftoff until January 16, 1962 and then postponed it again for a week later, on January 23.

On that date, hundreds of newsmen gathered at Cape Canaveral to witness and report the first U.S. flight into orbit. Astronaut John Glenn prepared to ride in the Mercury-Atlas 6 capsule, *Friendship* 7. Cloudy weather cancelled that flight and yet another launch attempt on January 27, 1962. Launchpad operations, technical problems, and bad weather delayed the actual launch until February 20, 1962. Glenn climbed into his capsule just after 6:00 A.M.

▲ Mercury astronaut John Glenn climbs into his Friendship 7 capsule. Each astronaut chose the name for his Mercury capsule; the figure 7 added to the end of the name reflected the number of original astronauts.

Shortly after 9:47 A.M. (local time) the three engines of the Atlas booster rocket ignited and lifted the launch vehicle off the pad.

OPEN HOUSE

Tens of thousands of people gathered in the area surrounding Cape Canaveral to watch the rocket disappear into the sky on a plume of smoke and flame. This first manned U.S. orbital launch offered a sharp contrast to the launch of the first Soviet cosmonaut from the nearly deserted launch site at Baikonur Cosmodrome ten months earlier.

INTO ORBIT

Glenn jettisoned the escape rocket shortly after takeoff. Five minutes plus a few seconds into the flight, the engines cut out and fell away, burning up in the atmosphere. Glenn was now in orbit, circling in a path that varied between 100 and 160 miles (160 and 260 km) above Earth.

Throughout his flight, Glenn performed status checks of the capsule's instruments but still found plenty of time to report on the view outside. He described beautiful sunsets, and in the dark night sky he recognized familiar constellations. Glenn also saw the city of Perth, Australia, brilliantly lit. The

> "I'm in a big mass of some very small particles that are brilliantly lit up. . . . I never saw anything like it! They're coming up by the capsule and they look like little stars. A whole shower of them coming by.
> **John Glenn, after seeing strange glowing particles—he called them "space fireflies"— fly past his window.**

▼ On February 20, 1962, the Mercury-Atlas 6 launch vehicle carrying John Glenn in Friendship 7 blasts off launchpad 14 at Cape Canaveral. Soon he is traveling at nearly 5 miles per second (8 kilometers per second) while orbiting Earth.

residents switched on all their lights in his honor. He practiced controlling the capsule's attitude manually and assumed manual control to overcome the effects of a sticky attitude-control thruster.

SEGMENT-51

After Glenn fixed the sticky thruster, other problems became apparent. A "segment-51" signal transmitted to Ground Control indicated that the landing bag for Glenn's capsule was no longer locked in position. The landing-bag design helped push the heat shield away from the capsule during landing so that it acted as an extra cushion for the landing.

If ground control could trust the segment-51 signal, it meant that only a pack of retrorockets held the heat shield in place. During reentry, these would break up and the heat shield would tear away. The capsule—with Glenn inside—would burn up like a shooting star.

Not wanting to alarm Glenn, Ground Control asked him to verify that the landing bag deploy switch remained in the "off" position—which it did. Only on his third and final orbit did they mention the segment-51 problem, saying that they suspected it was "an erroneous signal." But they advised him to keep the retrorocket pack on during reentry.

A REAL FIREBALL

During reentry, Glenn saw the orange glow as air friction heated the exterior of the capsule and noticed chunks of material hurtling past the window. Was the heat shield breaking up? As he approached Earth, the G-forces increased; temperature inside the capsule began to rise; was he going to make it? Flight controllers at mission control held their breath. Radio communications during reentry are impossible because radio waves cannot penetrate the

searing hot air surrounding the capsule. (A communications blackout like this happens whenever a spacecraft reenters the atmosphere.) Finally, the controllers heard Glenn report: "My condition is good, but that was a real fireball, boy!" He splashed down in the Atlantic Ocean about 40 miles (60 km) from the recovery ship. His flight lasted about four hours and fifty-five minutes.

▼ *After his triumphant three-orbit flight, John Glenn is hoisted from the recovery ship USS Noa to a helicopter that will take him to the USS Randolf to complete his debriefing for the flight.*

OUR HERO

The American people went wild over their new space hero. In the days and weeks following his flight, John Glenn was honored wherever he went. President Kennedy awarded him the Distinguished Service Medal; he addressed Congress; in New York, Glenn received one of the biggest ticker-tape parades (string confetti showering down from above all along the parade route) ever. He also addressed the United Nations. The U.S. now felt it matched the Soviet Union in the space race and became confident that it would soon surpass the Soviets.

UNFINISHED BUSINESS

Meanwhile, back at the Cape, Scott Carpenter prepared for a repeat three-orbit flight in his Mercury capsule, *Aurora 7*. He was scheduled to perform more science tasks than Glenn, including observing what happened to a balloon he released into space.

▶ *In a ceremony at the Manned Spacecraft Center in Houston, Texas, President John F. Kennedy honors John Glenn after his historic journey into space in* Friendship 7.

Just after 9:45 A.M. (local time), on May 24, Scott Carpenter's launch vehicle left the pad and placed him in orbit minutes later. He described the state of weightlessness he found himself in as "a blessing—nothing more, nothing less."

Just like Glenn's nail-biting reentry, Carpenter's reentry also turned into a cliffhanger when he experienced difficulty positioning his spacecraft for reentry. *Aurora 7*'s attitude-control thrusters almost ran out of fuel, and he manually fired the retrorockets several seconds later than planned.

As a result, he splashed down about 250 miles (400 km) off course and waited for three hours in a life raft before being picked up by helicopter. Carpenter never flew for NASA again. He became an aquanaut for the navy's SEALAB experiments.

JOHN GLENN (b. 1921)

John Herschel Glenn Jr. flew many combat missions as a marine pilot during World War II and in the Korean War. Afterward, he became a test pilot. He was selected as one of the "Original 7" astronauts in 1959 but left the space program in 1964, two years after his first flight. He served as a U.S. Senator from Ohio from 1975 to 1999. In October 1998, at age seventy-seven, Glenn returned to space on shuttle mission STS-95, taking part in age-related studies on how spaceflight affects body proteins and the body's biological clock.

▶ *Astronaut John Glenn photographs Earth from the Space Shuttle* Discovery *in 1998 while on his second journey into space—thirty-six years after his first spaceflight. His flight proves that age doesn't matter.*

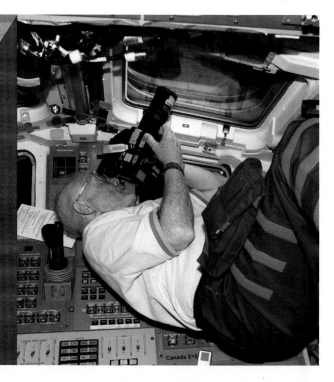

NASA
MANNED SPACECRAFT CENTER

UNITED STATE

UNITE STAT

▲ Scott Carpenter inside his cramped capsule Aurora 7, named after a street in his hometown of Boulder, Colorado. He was the second U.S. astronaut in orbit, and his flight lasted just four minutes short of five hours.

"Hola, amigos, felicitaciones a Mexico y especialmente a mis amigos de Guaymas. Desde el espacio exterior, su pais esta cubierto con nubes es muy bello. Aqui el tiempo esta muy bueno. Buena suerte desde Auror Siete.

Hello, friends, greetings to Mexico and especially to my friends of Guaymas. From outer space, your country is covered with clouds and is very beautiful. Here the weather is very good. Good luck from Aurora 7.

Scott Carpenter in orbit, sending greetings in Spanish to Mexico—and especially to his friends at the Guaymas tracking station on the Gulf of California."

Cooper's problems started on the nineteenth orbit, when his instruments indicated that the craft was decelerating, as if toward reentry. The automatic control system wasn't functioning correctly. After another two orbits, the system failed completely. Cooper had to perform a manual reentry. Despite the difficulties, he positioned the capsule and fired the retrorockets perfectly, splashing down only 1 mile (1.6 km) or so off target.

> "I could detect individual houses and streets in the low humidity and cloudless areas such as . . . the Tibetan plain and the southwestern desert of the U.S. . . . I saw what I took to be a vehicle . . . in the Arizona-West Texas area. . . . I saw a steam locomotive by seeing the smoke first . . . in northern India. I also saw the wake of a boat in a large river in the Burma-India area."
>
> **Gordon Cooper, recalling what he could see from orbit.**

▼ Launch Complex 14, long since dismantled, from which all the manned Mercury orbital flights left Earth for space. The monument honors the original Mercury 7 astronauts.

ADAM AND EVE

On June 12, 1963, NASA officially declared the Mercury program over. Two days later, the Soviets launched *Vostok 5*, carrying Valery Bykovsky.

▲ First woman in space, Valentina Tereshkova, in her space suit. No other woman followed her into space for nineteen years. In 1964, Tereshkova married fellow cosmonaut Andrian Nikolayev, who piloted Vostok 3. A year later, she gave birth to a daughter, Yelena, hailed as the world's first "space baby."

Rumors circulated that another spacecraft—piloted by a woman—would launch shortly afterward.

Sure enough: On June 16, *Vostok 6* carried Valentina Tereshkova into orbit. The two spacecraft came within 3 miles (5 km) of each other during *Vostok 6*'s first orbit. Some newspapers called the two cosmonauts the "Adam and Eve of Space."

Tereshkova spent nearly three days in space, returning on June 19, 1963. She remained the only female space traveler until 1982, when Svetlana Savitskaya flew into orbit in a Soyuz spacecraft. Bykovsky returned to Earth on the same day as Tereshkova after a record-breaking flight of four days, twenty-three hours.

THE WAY AHEAD

The flight of *Vostok 6* signaled the end of the Vostok program. The Soviet Union secretly pushed ahead with plans to launch a cosmonaut to the Moon, using an as-yet-unfinished Soyuz spacecraft.

The U.S. carried out its plans for an Apollo Moon-landing mission while the world watched. An intermediate program, called Gemini, in which pairs of astronauts would acquire the necessary flight experience to make a Moon landing feasible,

followed the Mercury program. An unmanned Gemini flight took place in April 1964, with the first manned flight scheduled for the following spring.

SOVIET SUNRISE

Soviet Union premier Khrushchev decided to outdo the United States by sending a multiple astronaut crew into space first and issued orders to this effect. In October 1964, a craft called *Voskhod 1* ("Sunrise") blasted off from Baikonur. It carried not two, but three cosmonauts.

A stripped-down Vostok spacecraft, *Voskhod 1* carried neither ejector seats nor space suits. Space experts believe that it was one of the most reckless and hazardous missions ever attempted—but it would help continue the worldwide perception that the Soviet Union space program held the edge over its Cold War, space-race rivals.

PRESIDENTIAL SUPPORT

War hero, Pulitzer Prize winner, and at forty-three the youngest-ever elected U.S. president, John F. Kennedy was destined never to witness the culmination of the Apollo program he initiated in May 1961. On November 22, 1963, he was killed by an assassin's bullet when visiting Dallas, Texas. Moon rocket designer Wernher von Braun said of JFK: "He made the country feel young again."

▶ *President John F. Kennedy visiting the Manned Spacecraft Center at Houston, Texas, in September 1962. He just received a model of the Apollo spacecraft command module. On his left is Vice President Lyndon B. Johnson, who succeeded him as president. After Johnson's own death, the Manned Spacecraft Center was renamed the Lyndon B. Johnson Space Center, in honor of Johnson, an enthusiastic supporter of the U.S. space program.*

CHAPTER FOUR

THE SPACE TWINS

In 1965, U.S. astronauts began orbiting the Earth in crews of two aboard Gemini spacecraft. The success of the first two flights was repeated by the eight Gemini missions that followed.

Gemini is the constellation of the zodiac called "the Twins." NASA chose this name for the second generation of U.S. manned spacecraft designed to carry two astronauts at once.

Even so, the Soviets, not the Americans, launched the first space twins. On March 18, 1965, just five days before NASA's first manned Gemini launch, *Voskhod 2* sped into space. On the second orbit of that mission, cosmonaut Alexei Leonov emerged from the spacecraft into open space to make the

"I looked through . . . the glass of the space suit. The stars were bright and unblinking. I could distinguish clearly the Black Sea with its very black water and the Caucasian coastline. One could even see what the weather was like there—I saw the mountains with their snow tops looking through the cloud blanket.
Alexei Leonov, recalling his ground-breaking space walk."

▶ On March 18, 1965, Alexei Leonov makes the first space walk of the Space Age. He said: "I felt absolutely free, soaring like a bird as though I was flying by my own efforts."

ALEXEI LEONOV (b. 1934)

Pioneer space walker Alexei Arkipovich Leonov made two flights in space, in 1965 on *Voskhod 2* and in 1975 on board *Soyuz 19*. The latter spacecraft linked up with an Apollo module for the *Apollo-Soyuz Test Project (ASTP)* mission. A noted and prolific artist, he produced sketches, cartoons, and paintings, often on space themes. An early ambition of his was to be the first man to set foot on the Moon—but it was not to be.

▼ *Alexei Leonov, pictured inside the Soyuz spacecraft during the Apollo-Soyuz Test Project in 1975.*

Gemini spacecraft, *Gemini 3*, crewed by Gus Grissom and John Young. Grissom spent so much time fussing over the spacecraft that workers nicknamed it the "Gusmobile."

The Gemini capsule had the same bell shape as the Mercury craft, but it was bigger, with space for two astronauts. It also differed in having opening hatches over the pilots' seats so that they could exit the craft for EVA. Another Gemini innovation was a guidance computer—the first ever used in a spacecraft—that was designed to help the crew navigate in space.

Unlike Mercury, the capsule formed only part of the spacecraft. The capsule, now called the reentry

first space walk, or EVA (extravehicular activity). It proved yet another propaganda exercise by the Soviet Union; the U.S. had planned a space walk for the second Gemini flight a few months in the future.

Leonov's ten-minute EVA almost ended in disaster when his space suit ballooned so much that he could hardly squeeze back through *Voskhod*'s air lock. Only by reducing his suit pressure to a near-dangerous level did he succeed in reentering the craft.

THE GUSMOBILE

As Leonov stepped out into space for the first time, technicians at Cape Canaveral made the final preparations for the launch of the first manned

▲ *The crew of* Gemini 3, *rookie astronaut John Young (left) and Gus Grissom. Grissom was the first person to make a second spaceflight. It would also be his last.*

module, was joined to a module that stored the retrorockets. This module, in turn, linked with an equipment (or adapter) module that housed the spacecraft's systems, propellants, and water supplies. The nose of the spacecraft was designed for docking, or linking up with another spacecraft in orbit.

ON THE BACKS OF TITANS

Overall, the Gemini spacecraft measured 18.4 feet (5.6 m) long with a maximum diameter of 10 feet (3.05 m). Made up of more than 1,200,000 parts, its mass in orbit was about 8,000 pounds (3,630 kg). The Gemini spacecraft was much heavier than the Mercury capsule and required a more powerful rocket booster to lift it into orbit. A modified Titan ICBM (intercontinental ballistic missile) served as its booster rocket, and the complete launch vehicle was called the Gemini-Titan. It stood 109 feet (33 m) high on the launchpad.

LIFTOFF!

Grissom and Young lifted off in *Gemini 3* on March 23, 1965. They were aiming for three orbits of Earth. Their primary mission was to "man-rate" the Gemini-Titan combination: that is, to make sure that it was fit to carry astronauts on longer missions. Grissom and Young tested the personal hygiene system and evaluated biomedical gear. The astronauts also notched a technical space "first." Using their on-board computer, they practiced maneuvers to change their orbit, something never attempted before.

One change took them as low as about 50 miles (80 km), to the upper fringes of the atmosphere.

▶ *A Gemini-Titan launch vehicle thunders into the air in January 1965 on a second unmanned test flight. This provided a comprehensive checkout of spacecraft systems and launch and recovery procedures.*

Named for the Broadway musical *The Unsinkable Molly Brown*, the *Gemini 3* was the only Gemini spacecraft that had an official name: *Molly Brown*. Grissom chose this name because his Mercury spacecraft, the *Liberty Bell 7*, sank shortly after splashdown on July 21, 1961. It was located in 1998 and raised from the ocean bottom in 1999.

▼ *The Gemini 3 capsule is hauled aboard the recovery ship USS Intrepid on March 23, 1965. The highly successful three-orbit flight blazed the trail for the nine Gemini missions that would follow. At the program's end, U.S. astronauts would be ready for the "giant leap for mankind"—a landing on the Moon.*

▲ *The distinctive black-and-white Gemini capsule. The crew capsule was black; the two other sections—the retromodule and the equipment module—were white.*

Near the end of the third orbit, reentry maneuvers began. The *Molly Brown* was properly oriented and the adapter section fell away, exposing the retrorockets. After those fired as planned, the retromodule was jettisoned. The *Gemini 3* capsule plunged through the atmosphere, heat shield blazing, then parachuted to Earth in a horizontal position. It splashed down in the Atlantic Ocean about 60 miles (100 km) off target.

> "Gemini may be a good spacecraft, but she's a lousy ship!
> **Gus Grissom, after being seasick while waiting for the recovery ship.**

LITTLE EVA

Astronauts James McDivitt and Edward White crewed the second manned Gemini flight, *Gemini 4*. On the flight, White hoped to perform the first U.S. space walk, or EVA. Because of that, NASA workers nicknamed the spacecraft "Little Eva."

Other "firsts" associated with this mission included the following procedures: On the ground, the Mission Operations Control Room at the newly completed Manned Spacecraft Center at Houston, Texas, would control in-flight operations. In orbit, the astronauts planned to attempt a rendezvous with the upper stage of its Titan booster. This space rendezvous was a primary Gemini objective.

Gemini 4 thundered into the sky on June 3, 1965. For the first time, the liftoff was broadcast live in twelve European countries via the *Intelsat 1 ("Early Bird")* communications satellite, which had been launched into geostationary orbit above the Atlantic Ocean two months earlier. (In a geostationary orbit, a satellite circles at the same speed as Earth turns and appears to remain in a fixed position in the sky.)

McDivitt's first task in orbit was a rendezvous with the Titan booster. He needed to maneuver in close and then fly in formation with it. The task proved surprisingly difficult—the astronauts found some of the maneuvers harder than anticipated. Because the attempts consumed too much fuel, mission controllers told McDivitt to knock it off.

FLOATING IN SPACE

The astronauts spent their second orbit preparing for White's space walk. They checked their space suits for leaks and depressurized the cabin so that it was airless, like space. On their third orbit, White opened the hatch above his seat and floated out into space. Only the umbilical hose—a tube that supplied

▲ Gemini 4 *blasts off the launchpad at Cape Canaveral on June 3, 1965, on the most ambitious mission so far of the U.S. space program. Its goals include the first U.S. space walk and a flight lasting more than four days.*

> This is the greatest experience, it's just tremendous. Right now I'm standing on my head and I'm looking right down and looks like we're coming up on the coast of California.
> **Edward White, speaking during his space walk.**

oxygen to his suit—and the attached safety line, or tether, connected him to the Gemini spacecraft. White carried a camera and a jet "gun," officially called a handheld maneuvering unit, to help control his movements.

White reveled in the new experience, rolling and tumbling and performing weightless gymnastics, first by firing the maneuvering unit, then by

tugging at the tether. When ordered in after twenty-one minutes, White called it "the saddest moment of my life." By comparison, the rest of the flight proved anticlimatic. But by the time *Gemini 4* splashed down on June 7, the astronauts had been in space for more than four days, nearly equaling cosmonaut Bykovsky's feat two years before.

ED WHITE (1930–1967)

First U.S. space walker Edward Higgins White was born in San Antonio, Texas. *Gemini 4* was his only flight. White was later selected to be one of the astronauts to fly on the first Apollo mission, *Apollo 1*. Tragically, he and his fellow crew members (Gus Grissom and Roger Chaffee) died in a flash fire on January 27, 1967. The flames completely destroyed the *Apollo 1* capsule during a simulated countdown while on the launchpad at Cape Canaveral.

▼ *More than 100 miles (160 km) above Earth, Gemini 4 pilot Edward White makes a spectacular space walk on June 3, 1965. The jet "gun" in his right hand fires to help him maneuver in outer space.*

CHAPTER FIVE

ACHIEVING OBJECTIVES

By the time the Gemini program ended in December 1966, the astronauts had logged more than eighty man-hours in space and had achieved all the program objectives, including long-term flights, space rendezvous, docking, and EVAs.

Gemini 3 and *Gemini 4*, like the Mercury capsules before them, carried silver-zinc batteries that provided electrical power for the spacecraft instruments and systems. This limited the mission's length to about four days—until the batteries ran down.

NASA engineers used fuel cells, a new source of electrical power, for the longer-term Gemini flights. A fuel cell works by means of a simple chemical reaction between hydrogen and oxygen that produces electricity, similar to the chemical reaction that occurs inside the dry cell batteries in your iPod. A fuel cell combines hydrogen and oxygen in the presence of a catalyst (a substance that accelerates the reaction). The reaction forms water, and in the process, produces electricity. Fuel cells made their space debut on *Gemini 5* and have been used routinely on manned space flights ever since.

EIGHT DAYS OR BUST

Crewed by Gordon Cooper and Charles ("Pete") Conrad, *Gemini 5* blasted into space on August 21,

▲ *The facilities at launchpad 19 at Cape Canaveral, from which all the Gemini missions were launched. The main access tower (left) is being moved in preparation for the launch of* Gemini 5 *on August 21, 1965.*

1965, aiming to spend more than a week in space. It was fitted with a rendezvous radar system so that the crew could practice rendezvous maneuvers with a radar target, called the radar evaluation pod (REP), ejected from the spacecraft.

Cooper released the REP on the second orbit and easily locked onto it with the rendezvous radar. But he stopped rendezvous operations because a

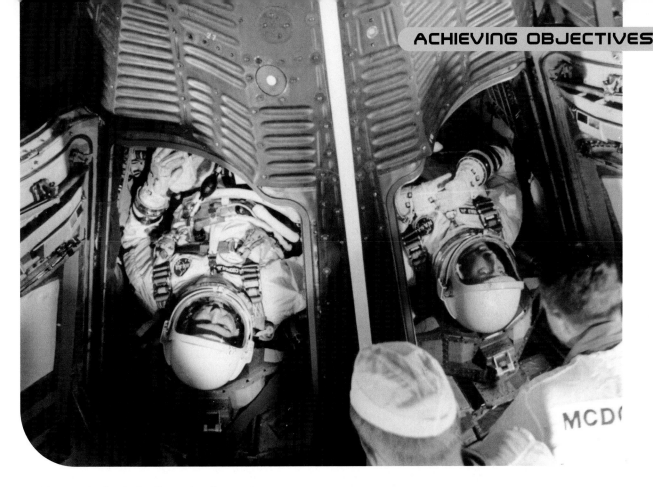

problem with the fuel cells surfaced. Oxygen pressure in the cells fell to unacceptably low levels, threatening the spacecraft's power supply.

If this continued, the astronauts would have to cut short the mission—and soon. By the fifth orbit, however, the pressure stabilized, and the crew got the "all clear" to continue their flight. They went back to practicing rendezvous maneuvers, this time using a "phantom target"—a particular point in space—aided by the onboard computer.

BREAKING RECORDS

On August 26, near the end of their seventy-fifth orbit, Gemini's crew smashed Bykovsky's four day, twenty-three hour space endurance record. And on they went. They were on the brink of achieving the mission objective of eight days in space until the last few hours. Out in the Atlantic Ocean, Hurricane Betsy was headed toward the splashdown

▲ Gemini 5 *astronauts Pete Conrad (left) and Gordon Cooper settle into their couches in the spacecraft prior to launch. They hoped to set a new space record of eight days in orbit but missed their target by sixty-five minutes.*

CREW PATCHES

Ever since the *Gemini 5* mission, each manned spaceflight had its own official crew patch, or emblem. Crew members got to choose the design. NASA decided to allow the astronauts to personalize their flights in this way after a concerted plea by Cooper and Conrad. The covered wagon motif they chose for the *Gemini 5* patch symbolizes the pioneering nature of the flight. Scheduled for a record eight days, the mission ended early because of a hurricane in the splashdown zone.

point. Mission controllers decided to bring down the spacecraft one orbit early. It splashed down after seven days, twenty-two hours, and fifty-five minutes.

Gemini 5's flight marked a notable turning point in the space race, signaling the moment when the United States surpassed the Soviet Union in total man-hours in space.

USING TARGETS

The key to a successful Moon mission lay in mastering the rendezvous and docking procedures of two craft in orbit. Gemini astronauts needed to perfect these techniques for the Apollo astronauts that would follow. NASA planned to launch an Agena rocket into orbit first as a target, and then launch *Gemini 6* an hour or so later to rendezvous with it.

On October 25, 1965, the Agena lifted off from the Cape but disappeared, probably after exploding and plunging into the Atlantic Ocean. *Gemini 6* therefore lost its target and was postponed. A few days later, NASA announced that *Gemini 6* would be launched in December, shortly after *Gemini 7,* and use that spacecraft as its rendezvous target.

▼ Gemini *spacecraft* 6 *and* 7 *make the first space rendezvous on December 15, 1965.* Gemini 6 *is pictured from* Gemini 7 *with Earth as a backdrop. The* Gemini 6 *crew spent three orbits chasing* Gemini 7, *finally closing in on it after seven firings of the thruster jets.*

▲ *Head-on view of the Gemini 7 spacecraft during rendezvous operations with Gemini 6. The crew set a new record by spending nearly fourteen days in space, during which time they circled the Earth more than 200 times.*

GEMINI RENDEZVOUS

Gemini 7 lifted off on December 4, 1965, with Frank Borman and James Lovell on board. They were attempting a marathon mission of up to two weeks in space—more than enough for a journey to the Moon and back.

The first attempt to launch Wally Schirra and Thomas Stafford in *Gemini 6* on December 12 ended only a second or so after ignition when the Titan launch vehicle malfunctioned. But three days later they were in space, chasing *Gemini 7*.

After four orbits and several intricate maneuvers, they "parked" *Gemini 6* about 120 feet (36 m) away

> You have moved us one step higher on the stairway to the Moon.
> **President Johnson, talking with the *Gemini 6* and *7* astronauts after their joint mission.**

from *Gemini* 7. The two spacecraft stayed together for about five hours, while the astronauts took turns maneuvering the two craft—which at one point approached to within 1 foot (30 cm) of each other.

Afterward, *Gemini* 6 returned to Earth after only about a day in space, but *Gemini* 7 completed its space marathon—just a few hours short of fourteen days.

▲ *On December 16, 1965, navy frogmen lend a hand to Gemini 6 astronauts Tom Stafford (left) and Wally Schirra after splashdown in the Atlantic Ocean following their sixteen-orbit flight.*

TROUBLES BEGIN

The Gemini program was moving along smoothly and efficiently, and when *Gemini 8* reached orbit on March 16, 1966, NASA held high hopes that it would achieve its two main objectives—the first docking in space and an EVA around the world.

After four orbits, the two astronauts, Neil Armstrong and David Scott, closed in to dock with the Agena rocket. They succeeded on the first attempt but withdrew when the docked spacecraft started gyrating. Although *Gemini 8* backed away, it continued to tumble wildly. Inside the capsule, Armstrong and Scott became so dizzy that their vision blurred and they could scarcely read their instruments. They tried to steady the craft by firing the thrusters of the attitude-control system, to no avail. The astronauts ended up switching them off and fired another set of thrusters designed for use during reentry. This time they succeeded and achieved a steady flight. All these extra thruster firings used up so much fuel that mission control ordered *Gemini 8* back to Earth.

THE ANGRY ALLIGATOR

The crew of *Gemini 9*, Thomas Stafford and Eugene Cernan, also experienced poor luck with docking on June 3, 1966. The outside cover on the Agena rocket target vehicle jammed and covered the docking collar. The malfunction made the Agena look like "an angry alligator."

▼ *The Agena target vehicle for the* Gemini 9 *mission shows the jammed payload shroud (outer cover) that made it look like an "angry alligator." The malfunction caused* Gemini 9 *to abandon its docking maneuvers.*

The second major objective of the mission did not go too well either. Cernan went space walking but found the experience hard work. He started sweating and his helmet visor fogged up—his suit's environmental control system could not cope. Nevertheless, Cernan set a new EVA record of more than two hours.

THE FINAL MISSIONS

John Young returned to space with Michael Collins aboard *Gemini 10*, which lifted off on July 18, 1966. It was an ambitious but highly successful mission. The crew docked with one Agena target and fired its engine to boost the Gemini/Agena combination into a higher orbit. Abandoning that Agena, they rendezvoused with another, and Collins went on an EVA to retrieve an experiment from it.

On September 12, 1966, astronaut Pete Conrad returned to space with Richard Gordon aboard *Gemini 11*. They docked quickly with an Agena target; later, Gordon went on an EVA to attach a safety line to it. The operation took so much effort that Young brought Gordon back in after fewer than forty minutes. As Young explained to mission controllers: "He got so hot and sweaty that he couldn't see."

Afterward, Young restarted the Agena's engine to boost the docked Gemini/Agena combination to

"The world is round! It's utterly fantastic. You wouldn't believe it. It really is blue. The water stands out and everything is blue. The curvature shows up a lot. Looking straight down you still see just as clearly. There is no loss of color, and the detail is extremely good.
Pete Conrad, on viewing Earth from *Gemini 11*'s **peak altitude.**

a higher orbit. It soared to a height of 850 miles (1,370 km), the highest altitude yet reached by a manned spacecraft.

The final Gemini flight, *Gemini 12*, which carried James Lovell and Edwin "Buzz" Aldrin, lifted off on November 11, 1966. In most ways, it was a repeat of *Gemini 11*'s flight. But Aldrin's remarkable feat of space walking distinguished the mission. He made no less than three EVAs, totaling

▼ *Edwin Aldrin on the final Gemini mission in November 1966. Fellow astronaut James Lovell called the mission "A four day vacation with pay, and you see the world."*

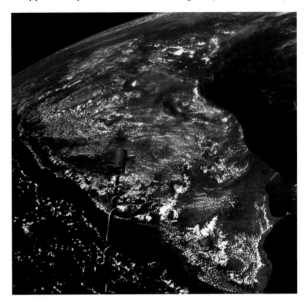

▼ *The Gemini astronauts took some spectacular photographs from space. On* Gemini 9, *the astronauts snapped this picture of India and Ceylon (now Sri Lanka).*

5.5 hours. No one knew it then, but Aldrin's next space walk would be on the Moon.

POSTSCRIPT

NASA's Gemini program was an outstanding success on several levels. In ten Gemini missions, twenty astronauts spent a total of more than 1,900 man-hours in space. This compared with a total of about 500 man-hours of time Soviet cosmonauts spent in space.

Flight after flight hit the headlines—White's spectacular space walk, the dockings with Agenas, the rendezvous between *Gemini*s 6 and 7. All captured the world's imagination. In the United States especially, many Americans hoped to fulfill President Kennedy's vision for a Moon landing.

But the Gemini flights also diverted public attention from some very serious political issues, including race riots that followed the Civil Rights Movement and the Vietnam War, in which U.S. troops became increasingly involved after 1965.

CHAPTER SIX

HEADING FOR THE MOON

Ten successful Gemini flights paved the way for the greatest space adventure of all time—the Apollo Moon missions. As probes searched for the best possible lunar landing sites, Apollo's engineers raced ahead designing the enormous and complicated hardware required.

The United States landed its first successful probes on the Moon in 1964 and 1965, when Ranger spacecraft returned close-range images of the lunar surface before crash-landing. In June 1966, *Surveyor 1* made a soft landing, five months after the Soviet Union landed an instrument capsule. Later Surveyor probes dug into and analyzed the lunar soil.

In August 1966, the first of five Lunar Orbiter probes began photographing the Moon from orbit. The high-resolution photographs helped NASA finalize the Apollo landing sites.

THE MIGHTY MOON ROCKET

The most impressive piece of Apollo hardware was the Saturn V launch vehicle. On the launchpad, with the Apollo spacecraft on top, it stood nearly 365 feet (111 m) tall and weighed about 3,200 tons (2.9 tonnes).

It was the biggest of a series of heavy launch vehicles that rocket designer Wernher von Braun and his team had been developing since the early 1960s.

Workers assembled the enormous Saturn V in a huge new building, called the Vehicle Assembly Building, or VAB. It became, and still is, the heart of the Kennedy Space Center. The VAB measures 716 feet (218 m) long and 526 feet (160 m) tall.

▼ *An Apollo 12 astronaut inspects the* Surveyor 3 *probe that landed on the Moon two years earlier, in April 1967. Surveyor sent back data that helped Apollo planners determine that the Moon's surface was stable enough to support a landing craft.*

▲ An Apollo/Saturn V stack on its way to the launchpad at the Kennedy Space Center.
This colossal launch vehicle never failed to deliver. Saturn V rockets launched two Apollo
crews into orbit around the Moon and six missions that landed on it.

THE APOLLO SPACECRAFT

The Apollo spacecraft consisted of three parts. The three-man crew traveled in the pressurized command module. Until the end of each mission, this was joined to the service (equipment) module. The third part was the lunar module, designed to carry two astronauts to the Moon's surface, lift off again, and rendezvous with the command module.

"FIRE IN THE COCKPIT"

By the time the Gemini flights ended in November 1966, the first Apollo flight was already scheduled for the following February. The *Apollo 1* mission crew members were Gus Grissom, Edward White, and Roger Chaffee.

On January 27, 1967, the astronauts performed flight simulations inside the command module. About five hours into the simulations, a frantic voice radioed this chilling message from the spacecraft: "We've got a fire in the cockpit!" Within seconds, flames engulfed the *Apollo 1* spacecraft. Boosted by its pure-oxygen atmosphere, the fire became an inferno inside the capsule; all three astronauts died.

As a result, NASA ordered many modifications to the command module, including redesigning the hatch for quick opening. This delayed the Apollo missions for more than a year and a half.

> If we die, we want people to accept it. We're in a risky business. And we hope that if anything happens to us, it will not delay the (Apollo) program. The conquest of space is worth the risk of life.
>
> **Gus Grissom, a few weeks before the fatal *Apollo 1* fire in 1967.**

▲ (left to right) Apollo 1 *astronauts Gus Grissom, Roger Chaffee, and Edward White during training. Their tragic deaths delayed the first Apollo flight until October 1968.*

SOVIET SORROW

Meanwhile, the Soviet space program faced its own difficulties. No launches occurred since *Voskhod 2* in March 1965. But Soviet space scientists were far from idle. They concentrated on developing new hardware, including the Soyuz and the related Zond spacecraft, for a voyage to the Moon.

Originally intended for manned Moon missions, these craft required a more powerful launch vehicle. The Soviets first flight-tested their D-booster in July 1965. Later, they renamed it the Proton—the launch vehicle still used today to ferry parts and supplies to the International Space Station.

Vladimir Komarov piloted the first Soyuz flight on April 23, 1967. The original mission plan included a second Soyuz that would follow and link up with *Soyuz 1*. In orbit, the docked craft would transfer their crews. But the second flight never launched. Instead, during his eighteenth orbit, the Soviets ordered Komarov back to Earth.

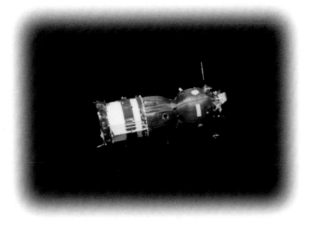

▲ An early Soyuz spacecraft in orbit. Conceived in the 1960s, Soyuz craft are still in operation, nowadays shuttling cosmonauts, astronauts, and supplies to and from the International Space Station.

Tragically, Komarov died during reentry. No one knows for certain what went wrong. The official explanation blamed it on a parachute failure that caused Komarov's capsule to smash into the ground at high speed, killing him instantly. He became the first in-flight casualty of the Space Age.

Within a year of Komarov's death, the Soviets were in mourning again—this time over the loss of their very first cosmonaut, Yuri Gagarin. Early on the morning of March 27, 1968, Gagarin took off on a routine training flight mission in a MiG-15 aircraft. Minutes later, the MiG stalled, plummeted to the ground, and caught fire; Gagarin died instantly. Ironically, the man who braved the unknown hazards of spaceflight died not on a space mission, but close to Earth in an airplane accident.

TURTLES TO THE MOON

NASA finally announced a revised schedule for its Apollo flights in August 1968. *Apollo 7*, the first manned flight, would launch in October, followed by a circumnavigation of the Moon by *Apollo 8* in December of that year.

This U.S. announcement spurred the Soviets into action—they were determined to beat the Americans to the Moon. In September, they launched *Zond 5*, with a live crew of turtles and fruit flies. It sped around the Moon and back, returning with live animals. On October 26, just four days after *Apollo 7* landed, the Soviets launched *Soyuz 3* on a successful, nearly four-day manned mission. Then in November, the unmanned *Zond 6* completed another perfect Soviet research trip around the Moon and back.

All the signs indicated that a cosmonaut crew in *Zond 7* would soon blast off for the Moon. Could the Soviets launch their craft in time to beat the *Apollo 8* mission scheduled for liftoff December 21?

For some reason, *Zond 7* never materialized, but to this day no one knows exactly why. That left only the United States with the goal of "landing a man on the Moon and returning him safely to Earth" before the biggest space race of the Space Age ended.

▲ An unmanned Saturn V rocket takes to the skies for the first time in November 1967. A little over a year later, another Saturn V launched the Apollo 8 astronauts on a journey that orbited the Moon.

1957

October 4: Soviet Union launches *Sputnik*. *Sputnik 2*, carrying space dog Laika, launched a month later. In December, a Vanguard launch vehicle explodes on the launchpad during the first U.S. attempt to put a satellite into orbit.

1958

January 31: First U.S. satellite *Explorer 1* launched. NASA established on October 1. The U.S. manned space program is named Mercury in December.

1959

First flights of the X-15 rocket plane, designed to investigate high-altitude and high-speed flight.

Soviet Union launches three Luna probes to the Moon; the first just misses, the second crash-lands, and the third photographs the Moon's far side.

1960

Soviet Union flies two dogs (Strelka and Belka) into orbit in a Vostok capsule and recovers them safely.

1961

January: United States launches chimpanzee Ham on suborbital flight in a Mercury capsule.

April 12: Soviet Union launches Yuri Gagarin in *Vostok 1* into orbit.

May 5: United States launches Alan Shepard on a 15-minute suborbital flight in Mercury capsule *Freedom 7*.

July 21: Gus Grissom makes an identical flight in *Liberty Bell 7*.

August 6: Cosmonaut Gherman Titov in *Vostok 2* makes the second orbital flight, spending more than a day in space.

1962

February 20: John Glenn becomes the first American in orbit in Mercury capsule *Friendship 7*. He makes three orbits of Earth.

May 24: Scott Carpenter in *Aurora 7* also completes three orbits of Earth.

August 11: Andrian Nikolayev launches in *Vostok 3* for a flight of nearly four days.

August 12: Pavel Popovich soars into space in *Vostok 4* for an almost three-day flight.

October 3: Wally Schirra spends more than nine hours in space in *Sigma 7*.

1963

May 15: The Mercury program ends after the flight of Gordon Cooper in *Faith 7*.

June 14: In *Vostok 5*, Valery Bykovsky spends a record four days, 23 hours in orbit.

June 16: Valentina Tereshkova becomes the first woman in space aboard *Vostok 6*.

November 22: President John F. Kennedy is killed by an assassin's bullet in Dallas, Texas.

1964
October 12: The Soviet Union launches *Voskhod 1*, with a crew of three.

1965
March 18: cosmonaut Alexei Leonov makes the world's first space walk from *Voskhod 2*.

March 23: Astronauts Gus Grissom and John Young perform a test flight of first Gemini spacecraft, *Gemini 3*.

The *Gemini 5* astronauts (launched August 21) spend nearly eight days in space. *Gemini 7* (launched December 4) and *Gemini 6* (launched December 15) become the first craft to rendezvous in space. *Gemini 7* completes nearly two weeks in orbit.

1966
Astronauts on *Gemini 8* (launched March 16) achieve first docking in space by linking their craft to an Agena target vehicle.

Eugene Cernan space walks for more than two hours from *Gemini 9* (launched June 3).

The *Gemini 10* astronauts (launched July 18) perform successful rendezvous and docking maneuvers with two Agena targets.

Gemini 11 (launched September 12) reaches a record altitude for manned spacecraft of about 850 miles (1,370 km).

Edwin Aldrin's three successful space walks from *Gemini 12* (launched November 11) helps mark the end of the Gemini program.

1967
January 27: The *Apollo 1* crew, Gus Grissom, Edward White and Roger Chaffee, perish during a training session when their capsule catches fire.

April 23: Vladimir Komarov lifts off on a test flight of a new Soviet spacecraft, *Soyuz 1*. He is killed a day later during reentry.

1968
March 27: Yuri Gagarin dies in a MiG-15 fighter jet crash.

October 11: The Apollo program, much delayed because of the *Apollo 1* accident, kicks off with the launch of *Apollo 7* into Earth orbit. It is the first U.S. flight of a three-man crew.

October 26: Soviet Union resumes manned flights with the launch of *Soyuz 3*.

December 21: A Saturn V launch vehicle speeds *Apollo 8* on the most daring journey of the Space Age so far—a circumnavigation of the Moon. Frank Borman, James Lovell, and William Anders become the first astronauts to leave Earth orbit.

atmospheric breaking
Using Earth's atmosphere to slow down a spacecraft.

attitude
The way a spacecraft is orientated, or positioned, in space.

capsule
The name given to early manned spacecraft.

communications blackout
The breakdown of communications between a spacecraft's crew and mission control that routinely occurs during reentry.

cosmic rays
Particles with high energy that travel through space.

countdown
The backward counting down of time until the launch of a rocket. "T minus 5" means five minutes before liftoff.

docking
The physical connection of spacecraft in space.

EVA
Extravehicular activity, meaning working outside a spacecraft in space; also called space walking.

G-forces
The forces astronauts experience when their launching rocket accelerates quickly. These forces are several times greater than G, the ordinary pull of Earth's gravity.

heat shield
A coating on the outside of a spacecraft that protects it from the heat generated during reentry into the atmosphere.

meteorite
A lump of rock from space.

mission control
The Earth-based control center that monitors the flight and crew activities of a spacecraft.

orbit
The path in space taken by a spacecraft circling the Earth.

probe
An unmanned spacecraft launched to explore distant bodies in the Solar System.

propellant
Rocket fuel that produces hot gases to propel the launch vehicle into space.

reentry
The period during which a spacecraft reenters Earth's atmosphere.

rendezvous
A maneuver that aligns spacecraft in identical orbits to achieve docking.

retrorocket
A rocket fired to slow down a spacecraft; used as a brake to reduce speed, dropping it from orbit.

rocket
A self-contained engine that carries its own fuel and oxygen to produce a stream of hot gases. As the gases shoot out backward through a nozzle, the reaction propels the rocket forward. Rockets work in space because they carry their own oxygen supply.

satellite
A small body that orbits around a larger one in space. Most planets have natural satellites, or moons. Earth now has thousands of artificial satellites—man-made spacecraft—that orbit around it.

stage
One of the rocket units in a launch vehicle.

suborbital flight
A flight into space in which a spacecraft does not achieve orbit.

thrusters
Smaller rockets on a spacecraft fired to help man.euver the craft in space.

trajectory
The path of a spacecraft through space.

weightlessness
A state of continuous free fall that occurs while in orbit when everything, including an astronaut's body, seems to weigh nothing.

BOOKS TO READ

Bilstein, Roger E. **Stages to Saturn: A Technological History of the Apollo/Saturn Launch Vehicles**. University Press of Florida, 2003.

Burgess, Colin, and Kate Doolan. **Fallen Astronauts**. Smithsonian Books, 2003.

Cullen, David. **The First Man in Space: Days That Changed the World** (series). WAL, 2004.

Dickson, Paul. **Sputnik: The Shock of the Century**. Walker & Company, 2001.

Donkin, Andrew. **Space Stories that Really Happened**. Scholastic Hippo, 1999.

Furniss, Tim. **An Atlas of Space Exploration**. Gareth Stevens, 2000.

Hall, Rex, and David Shayler. **The Rocket Men: Vostok and Voskhod**. Springer–Verlag, 2001.

NASA. **The Kennedy Space Center Story**. Updated regularly.

Stafford, Thomas. **We Have Capture**. Smithsonian Books, 2004.

PLACES TO VISIT

Johnson Space Center (Houston, Texas) www.jsc.nasa.gov/

Kennedy Space Center (Cape Canaveral, Florida) www.ksc.nasa.gov/

International Women's Air and Space Museum (Cleveland, Ohio) www.iwasm.org/

Intrepid Sea-Air-Space Museum (New York City) www.intrepidmuseum.org/

Neil Armstrong Air and Space Museum (Wapakoneta, Ohio) www.ohiohistory.org/places/armstron/

Oregon Air and Space Museum (Eugene, Oregon) www.oasm.org/

Pima Air and Space Museum (Tucson, Arizona) www.pimaair.org/

San Diego Aerospace Museum (San Diego, California) www.aerospacemuseum.org/

The Smithsonian National Air and Space Museum (NASM) (Washington, D.C.) contains the largest collection of historic air and spacecraft in the world, including the *Apollo 11* command module and a sample of lunar rock visitors can touch. www.nasm.edu/

Virginia Air and Space Center (Hampton, Virginia) www.vasc.org/

SPACE CAMPS

Florida, Alabama, and other locations host a number of space camps in the summer months. Lessons include learning about the nature and problems of spaceflight as well as "hands-on" experience in spaceflight simulators.
www.spacecamp.com
www.vaspaceflightacademy.org

WEB SITES

GRIN: GReat Images in NASA—View one thousand historic NASA photographs. http://grin.hq.nasa.gov/

The Kennedy Space Center archives—Research U.S. space history from the beginning. http://science.ksc.nasa.gov/history/history.html

NASA History—Read documents, hear sound bites, and watch video clips. http://history.nasa.gov/

NASA Kids—Information, games, and activities. http://kids.msfc.nasa.gov/

Space.com—Up-to-the-minute news about space exploration. www.space.com

Space Kids—Facts, information, and activities for tomorrow's astronauts. www.spacekids.com

Yahooligans!—A selection of good space sites for kids. www.yahooligans.com/Science_and_Nature /Astronomy_and_Space/

VIDEOS AND DVDs

Documentaries with archive footage:

***Apollo 8*: Leaving the Cradle.** Spacecraft Films, 2003.

Project Gemini: A Bold Leap Forward. Twentieth Century Fox Home Video, 2002. Docudrama

Apollo 13 Tom Hanks stars as Jim Lovell. Universal Studios, 2000.

ABOUT THE AUTHOR
Robin Kerrod writes on space and
astronomy for a wide audience. He
has chronicled space explorations and
achievements in such best-selling titles
as *Hubble, Apollo, Voyager,* and *Illustrated
History of NASA.* Kerrod is a former
winner of Britain's prestigious COPUS
science book prize.